The Dynamic Property Landscape

Author: Hannes van Zyl

Strategies for Success in a Changing Market

The Dynamic Property Landscape: Strategies for Success in a Changing Market

Email: Authorhannesvanzyl@gmail.com

Pretoria

Gauteng

South Africa

Contents

Introduction

I've never viewed myself as a particularly gifted Estate Agent. It often felt akin to learning to play the piano – despite countless hours of practice and numerous lessons, it simply didn't resonate with me, a sentiment echoed by many over the years. Perhaps my true talents are more aligned with writing, designing exquisite gardens, selecting the perfect colours and tiles for homes, and possessing a keen eye for fashion and fine cuisine.

My deep-seated passion for remodelling houses, coupled with the invigorating scent of wet cement, fuels my enthusiasm for the construction industry. I believe that creating remarkable developments and piecing together all the elements might be where I genuinely belong and where I did make a significant impact.

Therefore, I present to you a thoughtfully curated collection of my insights and diverse experiences, crafted for you to explore as you navigate your own unique path. Whether you're in search of inspiration or practical guidance, my hope is that this serves as a valuable resource to illuminate your way forward.

Acknowledgments

All the glory belongs to my Heavenly Father! I am truly grateful for the invaluable lessons I've learned and the wonderful friends I've made along this incredible journey of life.

It has been an absolute blessing and privilege to spend 25 remarkable years working closely alongside the most talented and dedicated Estate Agents in the industry. I sincerely appreciate all your efforts to help me grow and develop in this dynamic and ever-evolving field, which has presented both challenges and opportunities for growth.

To all the principals, I extend my heartfelt thanks for your kindness, unwavering support, and for granting me the opportunity to be part of each exceptional team that has become like family.

To the clients who have become dear friends, as well as those who have shown me that this path may not be the right one for me... thank you for your support, guidance, and the invaluable experiences we've shared together!

Chapter 1: Understanding the Property Market Landscape

Overview of the South African Property Market

The South African property market presents a complex landscape shaped by a myriad of factors that affect both residential and commercial real estate. This market is defined by its dynamic nature, with constant shifts in regulations, economic conditions, and property trends. Real estate agents, landlords, and buyers must remain acutely aware of these changes to navigate successfully. The evolving legal framework, often influenced by local government policies, plays a critical role in shaping market conditions, impacting everything from property valuations to investment strategies.

In recent years, fluctuations in the economy have contributed to a volatile property market. The repo rate, set by the South African Reserve Bank, serves as a crucial indicator of borrowing costs, directly influencing mortgage rates and, consequently, buyer affordability. As interest rates rise or fall, the demand for properties can shift dramatically. Buyers must stay informed about these changes, as understanding the implications of repo rate adjustments can significantly affect their purchasing decisions and overall market engagement.

Property trends in South Africa are continually evolving, influenced by demographic shifts, urbanization, and lifestyle changes. Buyers are increasingly drawn to properties that offer convenience, sustainability, and community features. For landlords, adapting to these trends is essential to attract and retain tenants. This includes understanding tenant preferences for amenities and living spaces that align with contemporary lifestyles. Real estate agents play a pivotal role in guiding clients through these trends, ensuring that they invest in properties that meet market demand.

The financial landscape surrounding property transactions in South Africa is intricate, marked by various financing options and tax implications. Buyers need to be aware of the nuances of financing property purchases, including the impact of various loan types and government incentives for first-time homebuyers. Additionally, understanding municipal rates and taxes is crucial for both landlords and homeowners, as these costs can substantially affect investment returns and overall affordability. Real estate professionals must equip themselves and their clients with knowledge about these financial aspects to make informed decisions.

Lastly, effective property management practices are vital in a fluctuating market. Landlords must develop strategies that address tenant rights and rental agreements while ensuring compliance with legal requirements. Understanding the implications of sectional title and body corporate regulations is essential for property owners in shared living environments. Furthermore, implementing security measures such as electric fencing not only boosts property appeal but also enhances tenant satisfaction. By mastering these elements, real estate agents, landlords, and buyers can navigate the South African property market with confidence, positioning themselves for success in an ever-changing environment.

Key Trends Influencing Property Values

The South African property market is influenced by a myriad of trends that shape property values and investment opportunities. One of the most significant factors is the ever-evolving regulatory landscape. Legislation surrounding property ownership, rental agreements, and tax obligations can change frequently, impacting both landlords and tenants. Real estate agents must remain vigilant and informed about these regulations to provide accurate guidance to their clients. Adapting to these changes not only ensures compliance but also offers a competitive edge in negotiations and property management.

Another key trend is the fluctuating market conditions driven by economic factors such as inflation, unemployment rates, and consumer confidence. These elements can lead to unpredictable shifts in property demand and pricing. Investors and buyers often need to analyse market trends to determine the best time to enter or exit the market. Understanding local economic indicators allows real estate professionals to predict shifts in property values and advise clients, accordingly, positioning them to make informed decisions.

Technological advancements are also transforming the property landscape, providing new avenues for marketing and property management. Digital platforms enable real estate agents to reach a broader audience, while property management software streamlines operations for landlords. Innovations such as virtual tours and online listings have become essential tools in attracting buyers and tenants. Staying abreast of these technological trends can enhance the efficiency of property transactions and management, ultimately influencing property values positively.

Interest rates, particularly the repo rate set by the South African Reserve Bank, play a crucial role in determining mortgage affordability and investment viability. As interest rates fluctuate, so do buyers' purchase power and overall market activity. Real estate agents must understand how these rates affect their clients' financial decisions. Providing insights on financing options and the implications of varying rates helps clients navigate the complexities of property transactions and investment strategies effectively.

Lastly, the impact of local government policies cannot be overlooked. Municipal regulations regarding zoning, development approvals, and property taxes directly influence property values. Changes in these policies can either enhance or diminish the attractiveness of certain areas, affecting demand. Real estate professionals need to stay informed about local government initiatives and potential developments in their markets to advise clients accurately and capitalize on emerging opportunities. Understanding these key trends is essential for success in a dynamic and frequently shifting property landscape.

The Role of Economic Indicators

Economic indicators play a crucial role in shaping the landscape of the South African property market, influencing both immediate decisions and long-term strategies for real estate agents, landlords, and buyers. These indicators, which include metrics such as GDP growth, unemployment rates, inflation, and interest rates, provide valuable insights into the health of the economy and consumer confidence. Understanding these economic signals allows stakeholders to anticipate market trends, making informed decisions about when to buy, sell, or hold properties.

One of the most significant economic indicators in the property sector is the repo rate, which directly affects mortgage rates and, consequently, housing affordability. When the central bank adjusts the repo rate, it influences borrowing costs for homeowners and investors. A lower repo rate typically encourages borrowing and spending, which can lead to increased demand for properties. Conversely, a higher rate may deter potential buyers, leading to a slowdown in the market. Real estate professionals must stay attuned to these changes to advise clients effectively and strategize accordingly.

Inflation is another critical factor impacting the property market. Rising inflation can erode purchasing power and affect consumer behaviour, leading to changes in property demand. For landlords, understanding how inflation affects rental prices is essential. Higher inflation may necessitate adjustments in rental agreements to maintain profitability, while also considering tenant affordability. Agents and landlords must remain vigilant of inflation trends to manage their portfolios and ensure long-term success in a fluctuating market.

Unemployment rates serve as a barometer for economic stability and consumer confidence. High unemployment can lead to decreased demand for housing, as potential buyers may hesitate to make significant financial commitments. Real estate professionals should actively monitor employment trends within their target markets, as an increase in job opportunities can signal a potential resurgence in property demand. By aligning their strategies with local economic conditions, agents and landlords can better position themselves to capitalize on emerging opportunities.

Lastly, gross domestic product (GDP) growth is a fundamental indicator of overall economic health, reflecting the performance of various sectors, including real estate. A growing economy typically correlates with increased property transactions and investment. Agents and buyers should consider GDP trends when evaluating potential investments or sales. By analysing the interplay between these economic indicators, real estate professionals can navigate the complexities of the South African property market, ensuring they remain adaptable and informed in a rapidly changing environment.

Chapter 2: Navigating Constantly Changing Regulations

Overview of Current Property Regulations

The property landscape in South Africa is shaped by a multitude of regulations that are constantly evolving. These regulations encompass various aspects of property ownership, management, and transactions, impacting real estate agents, landlords, and buyers alike. Understanding the current framework of property regulations is essential for anyone involved in the property market, as it influences everything from financing options to tenant rights and responsibilities. The landscape is influenced by local government policies, national legislation, and market dynamics, making it imperative for stakeholders to stay informed.

One significant area of regulation pertains to property transactions, which are governed by laws that ensure fairness and transparency. The Property Practitioners Act, for instance, has introduced new standards for real estate agents, emphasizing the need for ethical conduct and professional accountability. This act not only protects the interests of buyers and sellers but also aims to enhance the credibility of the profession. Additionally, understanding the legal aspects of property transactions, including the obligations of all parties involved, is crucial for navigating sales and leases successfully.

Landlords and property managers must also navigate a complex web of regulations related to tenant rights and rental agreements. The Rental Housing Act outlines the rights and responsibilities of both landlords and tenants, providing a framework for dispute resolution and ensuring a fair rental process. As the demand for rental properties continues to rise, compliance with these regulations becomes increasingly important for landlords to avoid legal pitfalls and maintain positive relationships with their tenants.

Financial regulations play a pivotal role in shaping the property market, particularly in relation to financing options and interest rates. The South African Reserve Bank's adjustments to repo rates can have a direct impact on mortgage rates and, consequently, on property affordability. Buyers and investors must stay abreast of these changes, as fluctuations can significantly affect purchasing power and investment strategies. Additionally, understanding the implications of municipal rates and taxes is essential for budgeting and long-term financial planning in property investment.

Finally, the impact of local government policies cannot be understated. Municipal regulations can influence zoning laws, development approvals, and property values. Stakeholders must be attentive to changes in these policies, as they can create both opportunities and challenges within the property market. By staying informed about current property regulations and their implications, real estate professionals, landlords, and buyers can navigate the dynamic property landscape more effectively, ensuring their strategies are aligned with the latest developments in the industry.

Compliance and Legal Obligations for Landlords and Agents

Compliance with legal obligations is paramount for landlords and real estate agents in South Africa, especially given the dynamic nature of the property market. South Africa's legal framework for property includes various laws that govern rental agreements, property sales, and the responsibilities of landlords and agents. Key pieces of legislation include the Rental Housing Act, the Consumer Protection Act, and the Property Practitioners Act, each of which outlines specific requirements that landlords must adhere to in order to maintain compliance and avoid potential legal disputes.

Landlords are required to provide safe and habitable living conditions for tenants, which involves adhering to health and safety regulations. This includes ensuring that properties meet the necessary building codes and that essential services such as water, electricity, and sanitation are functioning properly. Failure to comply with these regulations can lead to significant legal repercussions, including fines and civil claims from tenants. Additionally, landlords must be aware of the legal requirements surrounding lease agreements, including the clarity of terms and conditions, deposit handling, and the processes required for eviction when necessary.

Real estate agents also carry a significant responsibility when it comes to compliance. They must be registered with the Property Practitioners Regulatory Authority and adhere to the ethical standards set forth in the Property Practitioners Act. This includes the requirement to provide accurate information about properties, avoid misleading advertising, and act in the best interests of their clients. Agents must also ensure that all transactions are properly documented and that all necessary disclosures are made to potential buyers and tenants.

Moreover, understanding local government policies and how they affect property ownership and rental practices is crucial. Municipal regulations can vary significantly, influencing property taxes, zoning laws, and maintenance requirements. Landlords and agents must stay informed about changes in local government policies to ensure that they are compliant and that their investments are protected. Regularly reviewing these policies and seeking legal advice when necessary can help mitigate risks associated with non-compliance.

Finally, navigating the complexities of compliance and legal obligations requires ongoing education and awareness of market trends. As regulations evolve, so too must the strategies employed by landlords and agents. Engaging in professional development opportunities, attending industry workshops, and staying updated with legal reforms are essential practices for anyone involved in the property market. By prioritizing compliance and understanding their legal responsibilities, landlords and agents can enhance their reputations, foster positive relationships with tenants, and contribute to a more stable and trustworthy property market in South Africa.

Adapting to New Laws and Policies

Adapting to new laws and policies is essential for real estate agents, landlords, and buyers in South Africa, especially in a landscape characterized by constant change. The legal environment governing property transactions often undergoes significant revisions, influenced by economic factors and societal needs. Staying informed about these changes is crucial for all stakeholders in the property market, as non-compliance can lead to costly penalties or lost opportunities. This chapter will delve into the strategies necessary to successfully navigate the evolving legal framework, ensuring that professionals remain competitive and compliant.

One of the primary challenges faced by real estate professionals is the rapid pace at which regulations change. From property zoning laws to tenant rights and building codes, these regulations can impact property values and investment potential. Understanding the implications of new laws is vital for agents and investors alike. Regular training sessions, online courses, and workshops focused on legal updates can equip professionals with the knowledge needed to advise clients effectively and make informed decisions. Additionally, leveraging technology, such as legal databases and compliance software, can streamline the process of staying updated on relevant changes.

Landlords, in particular, must be proactive in adapting to new policies that affect rental agreements and tenant rights. The introduction of laws aimed at protecting tenant rights, such as the Rental Housing Act, requires landlords to revise their leasing strategies and ensure compliance with mandatory regulations. Keeping abreast of changes in municipal rates and housing policies can also influence rental pricing and property management practices. Regular communication with legal advisors and property managers can support landlords in adjusting to these shifts and maintaining a positive relationship with tenants.

Buyers in the property market must similarly adapt to changing laws that may affect their purchasing decisions. For instance, shifts in financing options, tax incentives, and government programs can greatly influence the affordability of properties. Understanding how new laws affect home loans and the implications of changes in interest rates is crucial for making sound financial decisions. Buyers should consider consulting with financial advisors to explore the best financing options available and to navigate the complexities of property taxes and municipal regulations effectively.

Overall, the dynamic nature of the property landscape in South Africa necessitates a commitment to continuous learning and adaptation among all industry players. By staying informed about new laws and policies, real estate agents, landlords, and buyers can position themselves for success in a competitive market. Emphasizing ongoing education, leveraging technology for compliance, and fostering relationships with legal and financial experts will provide a robust foundation for navigating the intricacies of the ever-evolving property sector.

Chapter 3: Fluctuating Market Dynamics

Understanding Market Cycles

Market cycles are an essential aspect of the real estate landscape that every agent, landlord, and buyer in South Africa must understand. These cycles typically consist of four distinct phases: recovery, expansion, contraction, and recession. Each phase presents unique opportunities and challenges that influence not only property values but also buyer and seller behaviour. Recognizing where the market stands within these cycles allows stakeholders to make informed decisions, whether they are investing in new properties, selling existing ones, or managing rental agreements.

During the recovery phase, properties that have been undervalued due to previous market downturns begin to see increased demand. Buyers often capitalize on lower prices, while investors look for opportunities to purchase properties that have the potential for appreciation. Real estate agents play a crucial role in this phase by providing insights into emerging neighbourhoods and advising clients on timing their investments. Understanding local market trends, such as changes in municipal policies or shifts in tenant preferences, can significantly impact success during this stage.

As the market transitions into the expansion phase, property values typically rise, and the demand for homes increases. In South Africa, this is often accompanied by a favourable economic environment, low repo rates, and increased consumer confidence. For landlords, this phase may mean an uptick in rental prices, while first-time homebuyers might feel pressured to act quickly to avoid missing out on desirable properties. Real estate professionals must stay informed about macroeconomic indicators and local developments to guide their clients effectively through this dynamic period.

The contraction phase can be a challenging time for all parties involved, as property values begin to stabilize or decline. During this phase, sellers may struggle to achieve their desired prices, while buyers may adopt a more cautious approach. It is crucial for real estate agents to provide realistic assessments of property values and to advise clients on strategies for navigating a slowing market. Understanding the implications of fluctuating repo rates and changing regulations can help stakeholders make strategic decisions that minimize risks.

Finally, the recession phase, while daunting, also presents opportunities for savvy investors. Properties can often be acquired at discounted prices, making it an attractive time for those looking to expand their portfolios. However, it is essential to proceed with caution and conduct thorough market analysis. Real estate professionals must equip themselves with knowledge of legal aspects surrounding property transactions, financing options, and local government policies to guide their clients through these turbulent waters. By understanding market cycles, agents, landlords, and buyers can position themselves for success, regardless of the economic climate.

Identifying Opportunities in a Volatile Market

Identifying opportunities in a volatile market is essential for real estate agents, landlords, and buyers in South Africa. The property landscape is characterized by rapid changes in regulations, fluctuating market conditions, and evolving trends. To navigate this complexity, stakeholders must develop a keen awareness of the market dynamics and remain informed about the latest developments. This involves closely monitoring economic indicators, such as repo rates, as well as local government policies that can significantly impact property values and investment potential.

One of the primary strategies for identifying opportunities in a volatile market is conducting thorough market analysis. This includes examining historical data, current trends, and future projections. Real estate professionals should leverage analytical tools to assess the performance of various property sectors, such as residential, commercial, and industrial properties. Understanding these dynamics allows agents and investors to make informed decisions about where to focus their efforts and capital, whether it be in emerging neighbourhoods or sectors poised for growth.

Networking and maintaining strong relationships within the industry can also uncover hidden opportunities. Engaging with other professionals, including mortgage brokers, property managers, and legal advisors, can provide valuable insights into market conditions and emerging trends. Additionally, participation in local real estate forums and associations can enhance knowledge and foster collaboration. Sharing experiences and strategies with peers can lead to the identification of undervalued properties or potential investment partnerships that might otherwise go unnoticed.

Investors should also stay attuned to regulatory changes that might open up new avenues for investment. For instance, adjustments in zoning laws or the introduction of incentives for first-time homebuyers can create favourable conditions for purchasing property. Understanding the legal aspects of property transactions is crucial, as this knowledge can help stakeholders navigate complex regulations and avoid potential pitfalls. By keeping abreast of policy changes, agents and investors can position themselves advantageously in the market.

Finally, embracing technological advancements can provide a competitive edge in identifying market opportunities. Utilizing data analytics, artificial intelligence, and real estate platforms can enhance market research and streamline property management processes. These tools can help track market fluctuations, analyse buyer preferences, and forecast trends, enabling stakeholders to make proactive decisions. By combining traditional market analysis with innovative technology, real estate professionals can effectively navigate the complexities of a volatile market and identify lucrative opportunities.

Strategies for Market Adaptability

In the ever-evolving landscape of the South African real estate market, adaptability is crucial for success. Real estate agents, landlords, and buyers must develop strategies that allow them to respond swiftly to changing regulations, fluctuating market conditions, and shifting property trends. One key approach is to stay informed about the latest developments in local and national legislation, as government policies can significantly impact property values and investment opportunities. Engaging with industry news sources, attending workshops, and participating in professional networks will equip stakeholders with the knowledge necessary to navigate these changes effectively.

Another vital strategy involves leveraging technology to enhance market adaptability. The use of data analytics tools can help real estate professionals monitor market trends and consumer preferences in real-time. By analysing data on property sales, rental yields, and demographic shifts, agents and landlords can make informed decisions about pricing, marketing, and investment strategies. Additionally, utilizing digital platforms for virtual tours and online property listings can broaden reach and attract potential buyers or tenants who may prefer a more convenient search experience.

Networking and collaboration within the real estate community also serve as significant strategies for enhancing market adaptability. Establishing strong relationships with other professionals, including mortgage brokers, property managers, and legal advisors, can provide valuable insights and resources. Regularly attending industry events and forums fosters knowledge sharing, allowing stakeholders to learn from one another's experiences and adapt their strategies accordingly. This collaborative approach can lead to better service for clients and improved decision-making processes.

Flexibility in financing options can further enhance adaptability in a fluctuating market. Real estate agents and buyers should explore diverse financing avenues, including traditional mortgages, government grants, and alternative financing solutions. Understanding the nuances of various financial products can empower buyers, enabling them to secure deals that align with their long-term investment goals. Additionally, landlords should consider flexible lease agreements that can accommodate changing economic conditions, thereby attracting a broader range of tenants.

Lastly, continuous professional development is essential for maintaining market adaptability. Real estate agents and landlords should seek ongoing training in areas such as property management best practices, legal aspects of transactions, and market analysis. By staying ahead of industry trends and regulatory changes, they can position themselves as informed experts in the field. This commitment to learning not only enhances individual capabilities but also ensures that clients receive the most relevant and effective advice in a dynamic property landscape.

Chapter 4: Real Estate Investment Strategies

Types of Real Estate Investments

Real estate investments can be categorized into various types, each presenting unique opportunities and challenges for investors in South Africa's dynamic market. Residential properties, including single-family homes, townhouses, and apartments, remain a popular choice among investors. These properties often yield steady rental income and can appreciate significantly over time, particularly in high-demand areas. Investors can benefit from the growing trend of remote work, which has shifted housing demands toward suburban and rural locations, allowing for potential capital growth in these regions.

Commercial real estate is another lucrative investment avenue, encompassing office spaces, retail units, warehouses, and industrial properties. This segment often boasts longer lease terms and higher rental yields compared to residential properties, making it an attractive option for seasoned investors. However, commercial investments come with risks, including economic downturns that can impact tenant ability to pay rent. Understanding local market trends and the economic landscape is crucial for success in this sector, especially in a fluctuating market influenced by consumer behaviour and technological advancements.

Real estate investment trusts (REITs) offer an alternative for those who wish to invest in real estate without directly owning properties. REITs are companies that own, operate, or finance income-producing real estate across a range of property sectors. They provide investors with the opportunity to earn dividends and benefit from property appreciation while maintaining liquidity. This investment type is particularly appealing for those who want exposure to the real estate market without the responsibilities of property management, making it a viable option for both novice and experienced investors.

Another emerging trend in the South African property market is the investment in mixed-use developments. These properties combine residential, commercial, and recreational spaces, promoting a live-work-play environment that appeals to modern consumers. As urbanization continues to shape property demand, mixed-use developments can yield diverse income streams and reduce risk through diversification. Investors should remain informed about local government policies and zoning regulations that can significantly influence the feasibility and profitability of such projects.

Lastly, the short-term rental market, driven by platforms like Airbnb, has gained traction in South Africa. This investment type allows property owners to capitalize on tourism and business travel by offering accommodations on a flexible basis. While potentially lucrative, it also requires careful management and adherence to local regulations, which can vary widely by municipality. Investors must navigate the complexities of rental agreements, tenant rights, and compliance with housing policies to maximize their returns in this fast-growing segment of the real estate market.

Risk Assessment and Management

Risk assessment and management in the South African property market is an essential aspect for real estate agents, landlords, and buyers. The dynamic nature of this industry, influenced by shifting regulations, fluctuating market conditions, and evolving property trends, necessitates a thorough understanding of potential risks. Identifying these risks involves analysing various factors, including economic indicators, demographic shifts, and legislative changes that can directly impact property values and investment returns. By systematically evaluating these elements, stakeholders can make informed decisions that align with their financial goals and risk tolerance.

One of the primary risks facing participants in the property market is regulatory changes. South Africa's real estate landscape is subject to frequent updates in property laws and municipal policies, which can affect everything from zoning regulations to tenant rights. Real estate agents and landlords must stay informed about these changes to ensure compliance and avoid potential penalties. This involves monitoring government announcements, engaging with legal experts, and participating in industry forums to gain insights into how new regulations may influence property transactions and management practices.

Market volatility also plays a significant role in risk assessment. The South African property market is affected by various economic factors, including interest rates, inflation, and global economic trends. Fluctuating repo rates can directly impact mortgage affordability and consumer confidence, leading to changes in buyer behaviour and property demand. Agents and investors should regularly conduct market analyses to forecast trends and understand the implications of economic shifts on property values and investment strategies. This proactive approach allows them to pivot their strategies effectively in response to market changes.

Additionally, property management practices are crucial for mitigating risks associated with tenant relationships and property maintenance. Landlords should implement robust screening processes to select reliable tenants, reducing the likelihood of defaults and potential legal disputes. Moreover, maintaining properties to a high standard not only preserves their value but also enhances tenant satisfaction and retention. Regular assessments of property conditions, adherence to safety standards, and effective communication with tenants are key components of a comprehensive risk management strategy.

Finally, financial planning and investment diversification can significantly reduce exposure to risks in the property market. Investors should evaluate various financing options available for property purchases, considering both short-term and long-term implications of their choices. Diversifying property portfolios across different types of real estate—residential, commercial, and industrial—can help mitigate risks associated with market fluctuations. By implementing a comprehensive approach to risk assessment and management, real estate professionals in South Africa can navigate the complexities of this ever-evolving industry and position themselves for sustained success.

Long-term vs. Short-term Investment Strategies

Long-term and short-term investment strategies in real estate are pivotal considerations for agents, landlords, and buyers navigating the dynamic property landscape in South Africa. Long-term investment strategies typically focus on holding properties for extended periods, allowing for appreciation and the accumulation of rental income over time. This approach aligns well with the cyclical nature of the South African property market, where fluctuations in demand and pricing can be smoothed out by a longer investment horizon. For instance, properties in emerging areas may initially yield lower returns but can significantly appreciate as infrastructure develops and communities grow, ultimately providing substantial returns for patient investors.

On the other hand, short-term investment strategies, often referred to as flipping, involve purchasing properties with the intention of renovating and selling them quickly for a profit. This approach can be lucrative in a rapidly changing market where property values are appreciating swiftly. However, it requires a keen understanding of market trends and a readiness to react to fluctuations in property values, repo rates, and consumer demand. For investors in South Africa, where regulatory changes can impact property values, short-term strategies may carry higher risks but can also yield immediate financial benefits if executed correctly.

The choice between long-term and short-term strategies often hinges on an investor's personal goals, risk tolerance, and market conditions. Investors looking for stability and steady cash flow might gravitate towards long-term holdings, particularly in areas with strong rental demand and stable tenant markets. In contrast, those willing to take on more risk for potentially higher short-term gains may find flipping properties in high-demand neighbourhoods or distressed markets more appealing. Understanding the nuances of both strategies can empower agents and landlords to better advise their clients, ensuring that investment choices align with individual financial goals and market realities.

Moreover, the impact of local government policies and regulations cannot be understated when considering investment strategies. Changes in taxation, zoning laws, and property rights can significantly affect both short-term and long-term investments. For instance, recent adjustments in municipal rates or body corporate regulations may influence operating costs for landlords, thereby affecting rental yields and overall property profitability. Staying informed about such changes is crucial for making strategic investment decisions that align with the evolving landscape of South Africa's real estate market.

Ultimately, successful navigation of the property market requires a balanced understanding of both long-term and short-term strategies. By leveraging expert insights and staying updated on market trends, real estate agents, landlords, and buyers can effectively position themselves to capitalize on opportunities while mitigating risks associated with market volatility. Whether pursuing a long-term investment for stable income or a short-term strategy for quick gains, informed decision-making will be the key to thriving in South Africa's dynamic property landscape.

Chapter 5: Property Management Best Practices

Effective Property Management Techniques

Effective property management is essential for navigating the complexities of the South African real estate landscape. A proactive approach encompasses a range of techniques that help landlords maximize their investment while ensuring tenant satisfaction. Understanding the nuances of property management can significantly impact rental income, property maintenance, and compliance with local regulations, which are all critical in a fluctuating market where regulations and demands can change rapidly.

One of the most effective techniques in property management is maintaining clear and open communication with tenants. Establishing a transparent line of dialogue can prevent misunderstandings and foster a positive relationship. Regular updates about property maintenance, changes in rental terms, or local regulations can enhance tenant satisfaction and reduce turnover. Implementing technology, such as property management software, can streamline communication processes, allowing for efficient handling of inquiries and maintenance requests, thereby improving the overall tenant experience.

Another vital aspect of effective property management is conducting thorough tenant screening. This process should include background checks, credit evaluations, and rental history assessments to identify reliable tenants. A well-screened tenant is less likely to default on rent or cause issues within the property, which can save landlords time and money in the long run. This becomes increasingly important in a market where the risk of default may rise due to economic fluctuations. By prioritizing quality over quantity in tenant selection, landlords can ensure a stable income stream.

Regular property maintenance is also crucial for preserving the value of the investment. A proactive maintenance schedule that addresses repairs before they escalate into significant issues can not only enhance tenant satisfaction but also reduce long-term costs. This includes routine inspections, prompt responses to maintenance requests, and staying updated on local compliance requirements. By investing in property upkeep, landlords can avoid costly repairs and ensure that their properties remain attractive to potential tenants in a competitive market.

Lastly, understanding the financial aspects of property management is essential. This includes keeping abreast of changing repo rates, municipal rates, and tax implications that affect profitability. Landlords should regularly review their financial strategies and consider seeking professional advice to navigate these complexities. Additionally, exploring diverse financing options for property purchases and investments can open up new opportunities and enhance cash flow. By integrating these financial insights into their management practices, landlords can better position themselves to adapt to the ever-evolving dynamics of the South African property market.

Tenant Relations and Retention

Tenant relations and retention are critical components of successful property management, particularly in the ever-evolving South African real estate market. With fluctuating economic conditions and shifting regulations, landlords must prioritize building strong relationships with their tenants to foster loyalty and reduce turnover. Effective communication is fundamental; landlords should establish a clear channel for tenants to voice concerns, ask questions, and provide feedback. Regular check-ins, whether through informal conversations or scheduled meetings, can help landlords stay attuned to tenant needs and preferences, ultimately enhancing satisfaction and retention.

Understanding tenant demographics and preferences is essential for tailoring services and amenities that resonate with their lifestyles. For example, young professionals may prioritize proximity to public transport and vibrant social scenes, while families often seek safe neighbourhoods with good schools. By conducting surveys or informal discussions, landlords can gather valuable insights that inform property improvements and marketing strategies. This proactive approach not only enhances tenant experiences but also positions properties more competitively in a fluctuating market.

In the context of a rapidly changing property landscape, offering flexible lease terms can be an effective strategy for tenant retention. Shorter lease options or the ability to renegotiate terms based on changing circumstances can appeal to tenants facing economic uncertainty. Additionally, landlords should consider providing incentives for longer lease commitments, such as rental discounts or upgraded amenities. This flexibility not only attracts a diverse tenant pool but also reinforces the landlord's commitment to tenant well-being, fostering a sense of community within the property.

Landlords must also be aware of the legal aspects of tenant relations, including the importance of adhering to rental agreements and local regulations. Understanding tenant rights and responsibilities can prevent disputes and enhance relationships. Regularly updating tenants on changes to property management policies, local laws, and market conditions can further build trust. Providing educational resources on tenant rights and responsibilities can empower tenants, allowing them to feel more secure and engaged in their living environment.

Finally, a strong tenant retention strategy should include a focus on community building within the property. Organizing social events, maintenance days, or community forums can foster a sense of belonging among tenants. These initiatives not only enhance tenant satisfaction but also encourage tenants to become advocates for the property, leading to positive word-of-mouth referrals. In a competitive real estate market, investing in tenant relations and community development is not merely a strategy for retention; it is a vital component of long-term property success.

Maintenance and Upkeep Essentials

Maintenance and upkeep of properties in South Africa require a comprehensive understanding of various factors that can impact both the value and functionality of real estate assets. For real estate agents, landlords, and buyers, it is essential to stay informed about the latest maintenance trends and best practices to ensure properties remain appealing in a competitive market. Regular maintenance not only enhances the aesthetic appeal of a property but also prevents costly repairs in the future, making it a crucial aspect of property management.

Understanding the local regulations regarding property maintenance is vital for compliance and successful management. South Africa's dynamic regulatory environment means that landlords and property managers must be aware of the legal obligations surrounding property upkeep. This includes adhering to safety standards, maintaining communal areas in sectional title developments, and ensuring compliance with municipal regulations. Regular inspections and proactive maintenance schedules can help property owners avoid legal complications and enhance tenant satisfaction.

The fluctuating market conditions can influence the types of maintenance that should be prioritized. For instance, during economic downturns, property owners might focus on cost-effective repairs rather than extensive renovations. Conversely, in a booming market, investing in upgrades can significantly increase property value and attract higher-paying tenants. Staying attuned to market trends allows landlords and property managers to make informed decisions about where to allocate resources for maintenance and improvements.

Investment in technology can streamline maintenance processes and improve communication between landlords and tenants. Utilizing property management software can help track maintenance requests, schedule repairs, and manage budgets effectively. Moreover, smart home technology, such as security systems and energy-efficient appliances, not only enhances the living experience for tenants but also reduces long-term operational costs. Understanding how to leverage these tools can provide a competitive edge in the ever-evolving property market.

Finally, fostering strong relationships with reliable contractors and service providers is essential for effective property maintenance. Establishing a network of trusted professionals can ensure that maintenance tasks are completed efficiently and to a high standard. Additionally, regular communication with tenants about maintenance schedules and updates fosters a positive tenant-landlord relationship, encouraging longer lease terms and reducing turnover. By prioritizing maintenance and upkeep, property owners can safeguard their investments and adapt to the changing landscape of South Africa's real estate market.

Chapter 6: First-Time Homebuyer Guidance

Steps to Homeownership

Achieving homeownership in South Africa requires a systematic approach, especially in a landscape marked by fluctuating market conditions and evolving regulations. Prospective homeowners should start with a thorough assessment of their financial situation. This includes evaluating savings, income stability, and existing debts. A comprehensive understanding of one's financial health will inform the budget for a potential home purchase. Additionally, it's essential to consider the costs associated with homeownership beyond the purchase price, such as maintenance, property taxes, and insurance.

The next step involves getting pre-approved for a mortgage. This process allows buyers to understand the loan amount they qualify for, which directly influences the price range of homes they can consider. In South Africa, various financing options are available, including fixed-rate and variable-rate mortgages. Consulting with a financial advisor or mortgage broker can provide valuable insights into selecting the best financing option based on individual circumstances and current market trends.

Once financing is secured, the search for the right property begins. This phase requires careful consideration of factors such as location, property type, and future growth potential. Buyers should stay informed about local market conditions, as these can greatly affect property values. Engaging with a knowledgeable real estate agent can facilitate the search process, as agents often have access to listings and insights that may not be readily available to the public.

After identifying a suitable property, it's essential to conduct thorough due diligence. This includes property inspections, reviewing municipal regulations, and understanding anybody corporate rules if purchasing a sectional title property. Buyers must be aware of legal aspects and potential pitfalls in property transactions. Engaging a real estate attorney can help navigate these complexities, ensuring that all legal documentation is in order and that buyers are protected throughout the process.

Finally, closing the deal is a critical step toward homeownership. This involves finalizing the mortgage agreement, ensuring that all necessary paperwork is completed, and paying any required fees. Once the transaction is complete, new homeowners should focus on settling into their property and familiarizing themselves with local municipal services, security measures, and community guidelines. By staying proactive and informed, homeowners can successfully navigate the dynamic property landscape in South Africa, turning their investment into a long-term asset.

Common Pitfalls to Avoid

In the complex and dynamic property landscape of South Africa, real estate agents, landlords, and buyers must navigate a myriad of challenges to achieve success. One significant pitfall to avoid is neglecting the importance of staying informed about constantly changing regulations. The South African property market is heavily influenced by local laws and regulations that can impact transactions, property values, and investment strategies. Failing to keep abreast of these changes can lead to costly mistakes, such as non-compliance with zoning laws or misunderstanding tenants' rights. Regularly engaging with legal resources and attending industry seminars can help professionals stay updated and mitigate these risks.

Another common pitfall is underestimating the impact of fluctuating market conditions. The property market is subject to various external factors, including economic shifts and changes in consumer behaviour. Real estate agents and landlords must be agile and adaptable, ready to adjust their strategies in response to market trends. Ignoring these fluctuations can lead to missed opportunities or financial losses. Conducting thorough market analyses and maintaining a flexible approach to pricing and marketing can help mitigate the risks associated with these fluctuations.

In addition, many stakeholders in the property market fail to recognize the importance of effective communication with all parties involved in transactions. Whether dealing with buyers, sellers, tenants, or other agents, clear and transparent communication is vital for building trust and ensuring a smooth process. Miscommunication can result in misunderstandings, disputes, and even legal issues. Establishing consistent communication protocols and utilizing technology for updates and feedback can significantly enhance relationships and streamline transactions.

Another critical area where pitfalls often arise is in financial planning and management. Many investors underestimate the importance of understanding financing options, repo rates, and associated costs involved in property transactions. Relying solely on intuition or previous experiences without thorough financial analysis can lead to overextending budgets or miscalculating potential returns on investment. Seeking the advice of financial experts and conducting detailed financial assessments prior to making decisions can help prevent these costly errors.

Finally, overlooking the significance of property management best practices can derail even the most promising investments. Landlords and property owners must be diligent in managing their properties, from maintaining physical aspects to adhering to legal obligations regarding tenant rights and municipal regulations. Neglecting these responsibilities can result in tenant dissatisfaction, legal disputes, or property devaluation. Implementing robust property management strategies and staying informed about best practices can enhance property performance and ensure long-term success in the ever-evolving South African property market.

Financial Planning for First-Time Buyers

Financial planning is a critical aspect for first-time buyers in the South African property market, especially given the complexities introduced by fluctuating market conditions and changing regulations. Understanding the financial landscape is essential for making informed decisions. First-time buyers must begin by assessing their personal financial situation, including income, savings, and existing debts. This assessment will help them determine how much they can afford to spend on a property while ensuring they have a comfortable financial cushion. Creating a detailed budget that includes potential costs such as transfer duties, legal fees, and ongoing maintenance expenses is essential for a holistic financial approach.

Next, first-time buyers should explore various financing options available to them. In South Africa, numerous financial institutions offer home loans tailored for first-time buyers, often with special incentives such as lower deposit requirements or preferential interest rates. It is advisable for buyers to shop around and compare different mortgage products, considering factors like interest rates, terms, and any associated fees. Consulting with a financial advisor or a mortgage broker can provide valuable insights and help buyers navigate the complexities of securing a loan that meets their unique needs.

In addition to understanding financing options, first-time buyers must be aware of the implications of current economic conditions on their purchasing power. The repo rate, for instance, directly influences mortgage interest rates, which can significantly affect monthly repayments. Staying informed about the Reserve Bank's monetary policy and its potential impact on interest rates is crucial. Buyers should also consider the current property trends in their desired areas, as market fluctuations can affect property values and investment potential.

Another important aspect of financial planning is understanding the legal implications of property ownership. First-time buyers should familiarize themselves with the legal processes involved in property transactions, including transfer duties and other tax obligations. Engaging with a qualified property attorney can help demystify these processes and ensure compliance with all legal requirements. Additionally, understanding the rights and responsibilities associated with homeownership, such as maintenance duties and local municipal regulations, can prevent future financial pitfalls.

Finally, it is vital for first-time buyers to cultivate a long-term financial strategy that extends beyond the initial purchase. This includes planning for future expenses related to property upkeep, potential renovations, and fluctuations in property value. Establishing an emergency fund for unexpected costs and considering investment strategies to grow their property portfolio can enhance financial stability. By adopting a proactive approach to financial planning, first-time buyers can position themselves for success in the dynamic South African property market, making informed decisions that align with their long-term goals.

Chapter 7: Financing Options for Property Purchases

Understanding Mortgage Types

Understanding the various types of mortgages available in South Africa is crucial for real estate agents, landlords, and buyers as they navigate the complexities of the property market. Mortgages can be broadly classified into several categories, each with unique features and implications for borrowers. The most common types include fixed-rate mortgages, variable-rate mortgages, and linked rate mortgages. Understanding these options not only equips stakeholders with the knowledge needed to make informed decisions but also helps them to advise clients effectively in a fluctuating market.

Fixed-rate mortgages are appealing for their predictability. Borrowers benefit from a consistent interest rate throughout the term of the loan, which typically ranges from 15 to 30 years. This stability allows homeowners and investors to budget more effectively, as monthly payments remain unchanged. In a volatile economic environment, where interest rates can fluctuate significantly, a fixed-rate mortgage serves as a safeguard against sudden increases in borrowing costs. This type of mortgage is particularly advantageous for long-term property investors who want to minimize financial uncertainty over the duration of their investment.

On the other hand, variable-rate mortgages offer interest rates that can change based on market conditions. While these loans often start with lower rates compared to fixed-rate options, they come with inherent risks. Borrowers may find their payments increasing if market rates rise, which can strain finances, especially in times of economic downturn or rising repo rates. For real estate agents and landlords, understanding the implications of variable-rate mortgages is vital when advising clients. They must weigh the potential for lower initial payments against the risk of future increases, ensuring clients are well-informed about their choices.

Linked rate mortgages also deserve attention as they tie the interest rate to a base rate, such as the prime rate set by the banks. This type of mortgage can offer advantages in terms of lower initial rates, but it also exposes borrowers to the potential for rate hikes. It is essential for agents and buyers to monitor economic indicators and government policies that may affect interest rates, as these changes can directly influence mortgage affordability. Adapting to these fluctuations requires a proactive approach to understanding how linked rates work in relation to market trends.

In conclusion, having a comprehensive understanding of mortgage types is essential for navigating South Africa's dynamic property landscape. With constant regulatory changes and economic variables affecting the market, real estate agents, landlords, and buyers must stay informed about their financing options. By equipping themselves with knowledge about fixed-rate, variable-rate, and linked rate mortgages, stakeholders can make strategic decisions that align with their financial goals and market conditions. This insight not only enhances individual investment strategies but also fosters a more resilient property market overall.

Government Assistance Programs

Government assistance programs in South Africa play a crucial role in shaping the property landscape, particularly in a market characterized by fluctuating economic conditions and evolving regulations. These programs are designed to support various stakeholders, including first-time homebuyers, landlords, and real estate investors. With the increasing cost of living and the challenge of accessing financing, government initiatives can provide essential resources to facilitate property transactions and investment, ultimately aiming to stimulate the housing market and promote economic growth.

One of the most notable government programs is the Finance Linked Individual Subsidy Programme (FLISP), which assists qualifying first-time homebuyers by providing a subsidy to reduce the cost of purchasing a home. This initiative has been instrumental in enabling lower-income individuals and families to enter the property market, thus increasing homeownership rates. Real estate agents and landlords should be well-versed in these subsidies, as they can significantly influence buyers' purchasing power and decisions. Understanding these options allows agents to better advise clients on financing strategies and navigate the complexities of property transactions.

Another essential aspect of government assistance is the provision of regulatory frameworks that govern rental agreements and tenant rights. The Rental Housing Act aims to protect both landlords and tenants, ensuring fair practices in rental transactions. Landlords must stay informed about these regulations to avoid potential disputes and legal challenges. By understanding their responsibilities and the rights of tenants, landlords can create more harmonious rental relationships, minimizing vacancy rates and enhancing property management practices.

In addition to direct subsidies and regulatory support, various government initiatives focus on improving the overall housing market. The National Development Plan emphasizes the need for affordable housing and sustainable urban development. This plan aims to address the challenges of urbanization and ensure that housing is accessible to all South Africans. Real estate professionals can benefit from this knowledge, as it helps them identify emerging trends and opportunities within the market. By aligning their strategies with government initiatives, they can position themselves favourably in a competitive landscape.

Finally, it is critical for real estate agents, landlords, and buyers to remain aware of the impact of local government policies on property values and market dynamics. Changes in municipal rates, zoning regulations, and development approvals can significantly influence property investment decisions. By staying informed about these policies and participating in local government discussions, stakeholders can advocate for favourable conditions that benefit their interests. This proactive approach not only enhances their understanding of the market but also positions them as informed professionals capable of guiding clients through the complexities of property transactions in a dynamic environment.

Evaluating Lenders and Rates

Evaluating lenders and rates is a critical step in navigating South Africa's dynamic property landscape. With the market constantly influenced by fluctuating interest rates, varied lending criteria, and changing regulations, it's essential for real estate agents, landlords, and buyers to understand how to assess lenders effectively. The right lender can not only offer competitive rates but also provide valuable guidance throughout the purchasing or refinancing process. Therefore, a thorough evaluation process should be established to ensure that all options are considered.

When considering lenders, it is vital to compare not just interest rates but also the overall costs associated with a mortgage or loan. Lenders may offer attractive rates but can include hidden fees, insurance requirements, and penalties for early repayment. Buyers should request a Loan Estimate from multiple lenders, which outlines all potential costs. This transparency allows for a better understanding of the total financial commitment. Additionally, evaluating the lender's customer service reputation is crucial; a supportive lender can make a significant difference in the often-complex journey of property acquisition.

Interest rates significantly impact the affordability of property investments. South Africa's repo rate influences lending rates, which can vary widely across different financial institutions. Regularly monitoring the Reserve Bank's announcements and economic indicators can provide insights into potential rate changes. For potential buyers and investors, timing their entry into the market based on projected rate movements can lead to substantial savings. Engaging with financial advisors or mortgage brokers who specialize in the property market can also help in understanding these trends and making informed decisions.

In addition to rates, lenders' flexibility regarding loan terms and conditions can vary significantly. Some may offer options like fixed or variable rates, adjustable repayment schedules, or special programs for first-time buyers. Understanding these options can help clients align their financial strategies with their property goals. Furthermore, lenders who have experience with specific property types, such as sectional titles or commercial properties, can provide tailored advice that addresses unique challenges and opportunities within those niches.

Finally, it's essential to consider the broader economic environment when evaluating lenders and rates. Local government policies, economic forecasts, and market demand influence not only property values but also lending practices. Staying informed about these factors can empower real estate professionals to provide sound advice to their clients, helping them navigate the complexities of financing in this ever-evolving landscape. Through diligent evaluation and strategic planning, agents, landlords, and buyers can position themselves to succeed in South Africa's dynamic property market.

Chapter 8: Navigating Rental Agreements and Rights

Essential Elements of a Rental Agreement

A rental agreement serves as a critical document in the property landscape, establishing the legal framework between landlords and tenants. In South Africa, where the property market is subject to fluctuating regulations and economic conditions, understanding the essential elements of a rental agreement is paramount for both landlords and tenants. A well-structured rental agreement not only protects the rights and responsibilities of each party but also minimizes potential disputes that could arise during the tenancy.

One of the foremost elements of a rental agreement is the identification of the parties involved. This includes the full names and contact details of both the landlord and the tenant. It is essential to ensure that the agreement includes a clear description of the rental property, including its address and any specific details that distinguish it from other properties. This clarity helps to prevent misunderstandings and ensures that all parties are aware of the exact property being leased.

Another critical component is the duration of the lease term. A rental agreement should specify whether the lease is for a fixed term or a month-to-month arrangement. For fixed-term leases, the start and end dates must be clearly stated. This information is vital for both landlords and tenants, as it defines the period during which the tenant has the right to occupy the property and the landlord's obligation to provide a habitable living space. Additionally, the agreement should outline the conditions under which the lease may be renewed or terminated, including any notice periods required by either party.

The rental amount and payment terms are also essential elements of a rental agreement. This section should detail the monthly rental amount, the due date for payments, and acceptable payment methods. It is advisable for landlords to include provisions for potential late fees or penalties to encourage timely payments. Furthermore, the agreement should address any utilities or services included in the rent, as well as the process for handling rent increases, which must comply with local regulations and market trends.

Finally, a comprehensive rental agreement should encompass clauses that address the rights and responsibilities of both landlords and tenants. This includes stipulations about maintenance and repairs, security deposits, pet policies, and rules regarding alterations to the property. Additionally, it should outline the procedures for dispute resolution and any applicable legal obligations under South African property law. By incorporating these essential elements, landlords and tenants can navigate the complexities of the rental market with greater confidence and clarity, fostering a more harmonious landlord-tenant relationship.

Tenant Rights and Responsibilities

Tenant rights and responsibilities are crucial components in the South African property landscape, influencing both landlord-tenant relationships and the overall health of the rental market. Tenants in South Africa have specific rights outlined in the Rental Housing Act, which aims to protect them from unfair practices and ensure safe, habitable living conditions. These rights include the right to a written lease agreement, protection against unlawful eviction, and the right to privacy within their rented premises. Understanding these rights empowers tenants to advocate for themselves and fosters a sense of security in their living arrangements.

On the flip side, tenants also bear significant responsibilities that are essential for maintaining a positive rental experience. They are required to pay rent on time, keep the property in good condition, and adhere to the terms laid out in their lease agreements. This includes respecting the property's rules regarding noise, maintenance, and alterations. Failure to meet these responsibilities can lead to disputes and even eviction, highlighting the importance of communication and understanding between tenants and landlords.

Landlords play a pivotal role in ensuring that tenant rights are upheld while also managing their own interests. They must be aware of their obligations under the law, which include providing a safe and habitable environment, addressing maintenance issues promptly, and ensuring that the rental agreement complies with legal standards. By fostering a respectful and transparent relationship with tenants, landlords can mitigate conflicts and enhance tenant retention, ultimately benefiting their investment.

The dynamic nature of the South African property market requires both tenants and landlords to stay informed about changing regulations and market trends. With fluctuating property values and economic conditions, understanding the legal landscape is vital for making informed decisions. Regularly reviewing local and national housing policies can help both parties navigate their rights and responsibilities effectively, ensuring compliance and promoting a fair rental environment.

Finally, education plays a fundamental role in enhancing the knowledge of both tenants and landlords regarding their rights and responsibilities. Property management firms, real estate agents, and legal advisors can provide valuable resources and guidance to help navigate the complexities of rental agreements and disputes. By fostering awareness and understanding, all parties involved in the rental market can contribute to a more stable and transparent property landscape in South Africa, reinforcing the foundation for successful and sustainable renting experiences.

Landlord Obligations and Best Practices

Landlords play a critical role in the South African property market, not only as property owners but also as key players in fostering tenant satisfaction and maintaining property value. Understanding landlord obligations is paramount, particularly in a landscape characterized by changing regulations and economic fluctuations. Landlords are required to comply with various legal obligations, including ensuring properties meet safety standards, providing necessary amenities, and respecting tenant rights. These obligations are not only legal requirements but also best practices that can enhance tenant retention and protect the landlord's investment.

One of the primary obligations of landlords in South Africa is to ensure that their properties are habitable and comply with the National Building Regulations and municipal by-laws. This includes maintaining the structural integrity of the building, ensuring that plumbing and electrical systems are safe and functional, and addressing any health hazards. Regular property inspections can help identify maintenance issues early, allowing landlords to make necessary repairs before they escalate. By proactively addressing these concerns, landlords not only fulfil their legal obligations but also demonstrate a commitment to tenant well-being.

In addition to maintaining the property, landlords must navigate the complexities of rental agreements. Clarity in rental contracts is essential to protect both parties involved. These agreements should outline the terms of tenancy, including rent amount, payment methods, and conditions for lease termination. Landlords are encouraged to discuss these terms with tenants to ensure mutual understanding and agreement. Furthermore, staying informed about changes in rental laws, such as the Rental Housing Act, is crucial for compliance and avoiding disputes. Clear communication and transparency in rental agreements can foster trust and reduce the likelihood of misunderstandings.

Another best practice involves timely communication with tenants regarding changes that may affect them, such as adjustments in rental rates or property management policies. Keeping tenants informed not only fulfils a landlord's obligation but also promotes a positive landlord-tenant relationship. Additionally, instituting regular feedback mechanisms allows landlords to gauge tenant satisfaction and address concerns proactively. This approach not only enhances tenant loyalty but can also lead to positive word-of-mouth referrals, which are invaluable in a competitive rental market.

Lastly, landlords should consider the financial aspects of property management, including the impact of fluctuating interest rates and municipal rates on their investment. Understanding the financial implications of property ownership is essential for sustainable business practices. Landlords should regularly review their financing options and be prepared to adjust their strategies in response to economic changes. Engaging with property management professionals or attending workshops on property investment strategies can provide landlords with the necessary tools and knowledge to navigate these challenges effectively. By adhering to their obligations and implementing best practices, landlords can thrive in South Africa's dynamic property landscape.

Chapter 9: Impact of Local Government Policies on Property

Understanding Municipal Regulations

Understanding municipal regulations is essential for anyone involved in the property market in South Africa, from real estate agents to landlords and buyers. These regulations serve as the framework within which all property transactions and developments occur. They cover a wide array of aspects including zoning laws, building codes, and land use policies, which can significantly influence property values and investment opportunities. As municipalities adapt to changing economic conditions and community needs, it is crucial for stakeholders to stay informed about these evolving regulations to make strategic decisions.

Zoning regulations are one of the most critical components of municipal governance, dictating how land can be used. For real estate agents and investors, understanding zoning classifications is vital when assessing potential properties. Different zones may allow for residential, commercial, or mixed-use developments, and knowing the limitations and opportunities of each can impact investment viability. For landlords, compliance with zoning laws is necessary to avoid penalties that could arise from unauthorized property use, affecting not only financial returns but also long-term property management strategies.

Building codes, another facet of municipal regulations, set the standards for construction and renovation projects. These codes ensure safety, accessibility, and environmental sustainability. When advising clients, real estate agents must navigate the intricacies of these regulations to provide accurate information on renovation possibilities and costs. For first-time homebuyers, understanding building codes can help in evaluating properties and making informed decisions regarding potential renovations or upgrades, ensuring that their investments meet safety and quality standards.

Moreover, local government policies can significantly impact property taxes and municipal rates, directly affecting the financial landscape for property owners. As repo rates fluctuate, landlords and property investors must consider how changes in municipal regulations could influence their overall financial strategies. Staying updated on rate changes and the rationale behind them can aid in forecasting potential expenses and adjusting investment portfolios accordingly. Knowledge of municipal rates can also empower property owners to challenge unfair assessments and engage in discussions with local authorities.

Lastly, the implications of municipal regulations extend to community development and infrastructure projects, which can alter property values over time. Understanding the local government's agenda and how it relates to property development can provide valuable insights for property investors. Engaging with community plans and attending municipal meetings can help real estate agents and landlords anticipate changes that may affect their properties. By fostering relationships with local officials and staying informed about policy shifts, stakeholders can position themselves advantageously in a fluctuating market, ultimately enhancing their investment strategies and property management practices.

Zoning Laws and Property Development

Zoning laws play a crucial role in property development, significantly influencing land use and the potential value of real estate investments. In South Africa, these regulations are designed to control how land can be utilized, ensuring that developments are appropriate for the designated areas. Understanding zoning classifications—such as residential, commercial, industrial, and agricultural—is essential for real estate agents and property developers alike. Each classification comes with specific guidelines that dictate what can be built, how properties can be used, and the density of development permitted in a given area.

In recent years, South Africa has witnessed a shift in zoning regulations in response to urbanization and the need for sustainable development. Municipalities are increasingly adopting mixed-use zoning to accommodate diverse needs within communities. This approach promotes the integration of residential, commercial, and recreational spaces, aligning with contemporary trends that Favor walkable neighbourhoods and reduced reliance on vehicles. Real estate professionals must stay informed about these changing regulations to advise clients effectively on potential investments, ensuring they are aware of the benefits and limitations associated with different zoning classifications.

The dynamic nature of South Africa's property market means that zoning laws can also be influenced by broader economic factors and local government policies. Economic fluctuations, like changes in repo rates, can affect demand for property and, consequently, influence local authorities' decisions on zoning amendments. For landlords and property developers, understanding these economic indicators is vital, as they can directly impact property values and rental yields. Keeping abreast of local government policies and their implications for zoning can help investors make informed decisions about property acquisitions and development projects.

Property buyers should also be aware of the implications of zoning laws when considering their options. Zoning regulations can affect the resale value of a property and its future potential for development. For instance, properties located in areas zoned for growth and mixed-use may appreciate more rapidly than those in strictly residential zones. Buyers need to conduct thorough due diligence, including reviewing zoning maps and understanding any potential for future amendments that could enhance or detract from the property's value. This knowledge empowers buyers to make strategic choices that align with their long-term investment goals.

Navigating the complexities of zoning laws requires expertise, making it imperative for real estate agents and landlords to stay updated on the latest developments. By understanding the intricacies of zoning and its impact on property development, industry professionals can better serve their clients and position themselves advantageously in a fluctuating market. Engaging with local planning authorities, participating in community discussions, and leveraging technology for real-time information can further enhance their ability to advise clients effectively. Ultimately, knowledge of zoning laws and their implications is a fundamental aspect of successful property development in South Africa's ever-evolving real estate landscape.

The Role of Local Government in Property Values

The role of local government in property values is a critical aspect of the real estate landscape in South Africa, particularly given the rapidly evolving market dynamics. Local government entities wield significant influence over property values through policies and regulations that govern land use, zoning, and development. These regulations can either enhance or detract from property desirability, affecting everything from commercial developments to residential neighbourhoods. Real estate agents and landlords must stay informed about these regulations, as changes can lead to shifts in property values that impact investment decisions and market strategies.

Zoning laws established by local governments dictate how land can be used, which directly affects property values. For instance, areas designated for commercial use may see increased demand and higher property values compared to residential zones. Conversely, restrictive zoning can limit development opportunities, stalling growth, and potentially lowering property values. Real estate professionals must understand the zoning landscape in their areas to advise clients effectively. Knowledge of upcoming zoning changes can provide insights into potential shifts in property values, allowing agents and investors to make informed decisions.

Local government infrastructure investments also play a significant role in shaping property values. Improvements in public transport, roadways, and community amenities can make an area more attractive to homebuyers and investors alike. For example, the establishment of new schools, parks, and shopping centres can enhance the liveability of a neighbourhood, leading to increased demand and appreciation in property values. Real estate agents should thus monitor local government budgets and planning initiatives to identify upcoming projects that could positively influence property markets.

Additionally, local government policies concerning property taxes and municipal rates can have a profound impact on property values. Higher municipal rates may deter potential buyers or investors, leading to stagnation or decline in property values. Conversely, favourable tax incentives can attract new businesses and residents, driving property demand and increasing values. Understanding the nuances of local taxation policies allows real estate professionals to better advise their clients and strategize for both short-term and long-term investments.

Finally, the relationship between local government and community engagement can significantly influence property values. Community input on development projects often shapes the direction of local policies, which in turn can affect the desirability of certain areas. Real estate agents and landlords should foster relationships with local government representatives and participate in community meetings to stay abreast of public sentiment and potential changes that could impact property values. By remaining engaged in the local governance process, real estate professionals can better position themselves and their clients to navigate the complexities of the property market effectively.

Chapter 10: Market Analysis for Property Investors

Conducting Market Research

Conducting market research is a fundamental step for real estate agents, landlords, and buyers in South Africa, especially in a landscape characterized by fluctuating regulations and economic conditions. Understanding the nuances of the property market can significantly influence decision-making and strategy formulation. Comprehensive market research enables stakeholders to identify trends, evaluate property values, and assess the potential impacts of economic indicators such as repo rates and local government policies. By leveraging this knowledge, professionals can better position themselves to navigate the complexities of the market.

The process of market research begins with data collection, which involves gathering quantitative and qualitative information about the property landscape. Real estate agents can utilize online databases, property listings, and local market reports to obtain current data on property prices, rental yields, and demand trends. Additionally, surveys and interviews with tenants and landlords can provide insights into preferences and expectations, allowing agents to tailor their services effectively. This dual approach ensures a well-rounded understanding of the market, facilitating informed discussions with clients.

Analysing the data collected is equally crucial. Real estate professionals must look for patterns and correlations that can indicate future market movements. For instance, a rising trend in property prices in a particular area might suggest an increase in demand, potentially signalling a good investment opportunity. Conversely, a decline in rental rates could indicate oversupply or changing tenant preferences. By employing analytical tools and techniques, agents can derive actionable insights that inform pricing strategies, marketing efforts, and client advisories.

Understanding the regulatory environment is another critical aspect of market research. South African real estate is influenced by various local and national regulations that can impact property transactions, tenant rights, and landlord obligations. Keeping abreast of changes in legislation, such as amendments to rental agreements or property taxes, is essential. This knowledge not only helps agents remain compliant but also positions them as trusted advisors to clients who may be navigating these complexities for the first time.

Finally, continuous market research is vital in a dynamic property landscape. The real estate market is not static; it evolves based on economic shifts, demographic changes, and technological advancements. Regularly updating market research practices ensures that agents, landlords, and buyers remain informed and responsive to changes. Engaging with industry reports, attending seminars, and participating in professional networks can enhance one's understanding of emerging trends and best practices. By committing to ongoing market research, stakeholders can maintain a competitive edge and achieve long-term success in the ever-changing property market.

Tools for Market Analysis

In the dynamic property landscape of South Africa, understanding market trends is pivotal for real estate agents, landlords, and buyers alike. One of the most effective tools for market analysis is comprehensive data analytics platforms that aggregate property listings, sales history, and demographic information. These platforms enable users to analyse trends over time, identifying which areas are experiencing growth or decline. By leveraging this data, stakeholders can make informed decisions about where to invest, how to price properties, and when to enter or exit the market.

Another essential tool for market analysis is the utilization of comparative market analysis (CMA). CMAs allow real estate professionals to assess similar properties in a given area, providing insights into average pricing, days on market, and features that appeal to buyers. This tool is invaluable for setting competitive prices, whether for selling a property or determining rental rates. By carefully analysing the competition, agents and landlords can position their offerings to meet market expectations and attract potential buyers or tenants.

In addition to data analytics and CMAs, geographic information systems (GIS) play a significant role in understanding property markets. GIS technology enables users to visualize data on maps, revealing patterns and trends related to location. This can include factors such as proximity to schools, public transport, and amenities, which are crucial for buyers and renters. By employing GIS, real estate agents can better advise clients on desirable locations and investment opportunities, thereby enhancing their overall service.

Market sentiment analysis tools, which gauge consumer opinions and perceptions, are also vital in a fluctuating market. These tools often analyse social media trends, online reviews, and news articles to provide a pulse on public sentiment regarding specific neighbourhoods or property types. By understanding how potential buyers and tenants feel about different areas, agents and landlords can tailor their marketing strategies and property features to align with current consumer preferences, increasing their chances of success.

Lastly, keeping abreast of regulatory changes and economic indicators is crucial for effective market analysis. Resources such as government reports, financial news outlets, and industry publications provide essential information regarding interest rates, zoning laws, and housing policies. By staying informed about these variables, real estate professionals can adapt their strategies, accordingly, ensuring they remain competitive and compliant in the ever-changing property market. This comprehensive approach to market analysis not only strengthens decision-making but also equips stakeholders with the knowledge needed to navigate South Africa's complex property landscape successfully.

Interpreting Market Data for Investment Decisions

Interpreting market data is essential for making informed investment decisions in the South African property landscape. The ability to analyse various data points, such as property prices, rental yields, and demographic trends, empowers real estate agents, landlords, and buyers to navigate the complexities of a constantly changing market. Market data can provide insights into the demand and supply dynamics of different regions, enabling stakeholders to identify lucrative investment opportunities. By understanding how to read and interpret these data sets, investors can make strategic decisions that align with their financial goals.

One critical aspect to consider when analysing market data is the impact of fluctuating economic indicators, such as repo rates and inflation. Changes in these rates can significantly affect borrowing costs and, consequently, property prices. For instance, a rise in the repo rate may lead to higher mortgage rates, which can deter potential buyers and put downward pressure on property values. Therefore, it is crucial for real estate professionals to stay updated on economic trends and understand their implications for property investments. This understanding allows them to advise clients on the best times to buy or sell and how to structure financing to mitigate risks associated with these fluctuations.

Furthermore, the influence of local government policies cannot be overlooked. Regulations regarding zoning, property taxes, and rental agreements can substantially impact investment prospects. For example, a shift in zoning laws might open up new areas for development, while increases in municipal rates could affect the profitability of rental properties. By closely monitoring these policy changes and their effects on the market, real estate agents and landlords can better position themselves to capitalize on emerging opportunities while minimizing potential pitfalls.

In addition to macroeconomic factors and regulatory changes, understanding property trends is vital for effective market analysis. This includes keeping track of shifts in buyer preferences, such as the growing demand for eco-friendly homes or properties with advanced security features. By recognizing these trends, real estate professionals can tailor their strategies to meet the evolving needs of buyers and tenants. This adaptability not only enhances their competitive edge but also ensures that their investments align with market demands.

Finally, data interpretation is not solely about recognizing patterns; it also involves forecasting future market movements. Utilizing historical data and market analytics tools can help investors anticipate changes in property values and rental rates. This forward-looking approach enables real estate professionals to make proactive investment decisions rather than reactive ones. By leveraging market data effectively, stakeholders in the South African property market can navigate its complexities with greater confidence and achieve sustained success in a dynamic environment.

Chapter 11: Taxes and Financial Considerations

Overview of Property Taxes in South Africa

In South Africa, property taxes play a crucial role in the overall real estate landscape, impacting both property owners and potential buyers. These taxes are primarily levied by local municipalities and can vary significantly depending on the location and type of property. Property taxes are generally based on the market value of the property, which is assessed periodically by municipal authorities. Understanding how these taxes function is essential for real estate agents, landlords, and buyers, as they can influence investment decisions and overall property management strategies.

The main types of property taxes in South Africa include municipal rates, which are charged for the provision of local services such as water, sanitation, and waste management. These rates are typically calculated as a percentage of the property's assessed value. Additionally, property owners may be subject to other taxes, such as the Capital Gains Tax (CGT) upon selling their property, which can significantly affect the net profit from such transactions. The nuances of these taxes require real estate professionals to remain vigilant and informed, particularly as regulations can change with little notice.

Recent developments in South African property tax legislation have introduced measures aimed at increasing transparency and fairness. For instance, the implementation of the Municipal Property Rates Act has provided a framework for how municipalities should value and tax properties. This has led to more standardized practices, but it also necessitates that real estate agents and landlords stay updated on their local municipality's specific regulations, as non-compliance can result in hefty fines or penalties.

The fluctuating property market also has implications for property taxes. As property values rise and fall, so too do the associated tax liabilities. In times of economic downturn, property owners may find themselves struggling to keep up with tax payments, which can lead to increased pressure on the rental market and overall property investment strategies. Real estate professionals must consider these dynamics when advising clients, ensuring they account for potential tax implications in their financial planning and investment analyses.

Lastly, the impact of local government policies and economic factors such as interest rates must be considered when discussing property taxes in South Africa. Changes in repo rates can influence borrowing costs, which in turn affect property values and the ability of buyers to enter the market. Understanding these interconnected factors is essential for real estate agents and investors alike, as it empowers them to make informed decisions that align with the ever-evolving property landscape in South Africa.

Implications of Capital Gains Tax

The implications of capital gains tax (CGT) in South Africa's dynamic property landscape are significant for real estate agents, landlords, and buyers. Understanding CGT is crucial as it directly impacts the profitability of property transactions. When property owners sell their assets, they may be subject to CGT on the profit made from the sale, which can influence both selling strategies and investment decisions. For real estate professionals, staying informed about the current CGT regulations and thresholds can aid in advising clients effectively, ensuring that both buyers and sellers are aware of their potential tax liabilities.

For landlords, the implications of CGT extend beyond individual property sales. Selling a rental property can trigger significant tax liabilities, which can alter the overall return on investment (ROI). This factor should be considered when evaluating the timing of a sale, especially in a fluctuating market. A thorough understanding of how CGT is calculated, including exemptions and deductions, allows landlords to plan strategically and optimize their tax position. Additionally, the impact of CGT on long-term investment strategies is a critical consideration, as it may affect decisions regarding property upgrades or the acquisition of new assets.

Real estate agents play a vital role in guiding clients through the complexities of property transactions, including CGT implications. They must be adept at communicating the nuances of the tax system, particularly how it may evolve with changing regulations. For instance, as government policies and tax laws shift, agents need to provide up-to-date information that can influence clients' buying and selling strategies. This not only helps in building trust with clients but also positions agents as knowledgeable professionals in a rapidly changing market, which can lead to increased referrals and repeat business.

For buyers, understanding CGT is essential in making informed decisions about property investments. Buyers should consider the potential tax implications when evaluating properties, particularly with regard to future resale. Awareness of CGT can affect the choice of property type, location, and the overall investment strategy. Moreover, first-time homebuyers must be educated about CGT exemptions and how these may apply to their specific situations, as this knowledge can significantly impact their financial planning and long-term property goals.

In conclusion, the implications of capital gains tax in South Africa's property market underscore the necessity for continuous education and expertise among real estate professionals. As the market evolves, so too will the tax landscape, making it imperative for agents, landlords, and buyers to stay informed. By understanding the nuances of CGT and its impact on property transactions, stakeholders can make better decisions that align with their financial objectives and navigate the complexities of the property market more effectively.

Tax Strategies for Property Owners

Tax strategies play a crucial role for property owners in South Africa, especially in a landscape marked by fluctuating market conditions and shifting regulations. Understanding how to navigate the tax implications of property ownership can lead to significant savings and a more efficient management of assets. Property owners, whether they are landlords, real estate agents, or buyers, must be aware of the various tax deductions and benefits available to them. Familiarity with these strategies can enhance cash flow, thereby allowing for reinvestment in other areas of the property market.

One of the primary tax benefits available to property owners is the ability to deduct expenses associated with property management and maintenance. This includes costs related to repairs, utilities, and even property management fees. Landlords, in particular, can take advantage of these deductions to reduce their taxable income. It is essential to keep accurate records and receipts for all expenses incurred in managing properties, as these can significantly lower the overall tax burden when the time comes to file returns.

In addition to operational expenses, property depreciation offers another avenue for tax relief. The South African Revenue Service allows property owners to claim a depreciation allowance on their investment properties. This non-cash deduction can offset taxable income, making it a valuable strategy for landlords and investors. Understanding the specifics of how depreciation is calculated and the relevant times for different property types is vital for maximizing this benefit.

Capital gains tax (CGT) is another critical consideration for property owners. When selling a property, the profit made is subject to CGT, which can impact overall returns. However, property owners can employ strategies to minimize their CGT liability. For instance, if the property has been held for a longer period, it may qualify for certain exclusions or exemptions. Additionally, reinvesting the proceeds into another property can defer this tax, allowing for continued growth in the property portfolio without immediate financial repercussions.

Lastly, staying informed about changes in tax regulations and government policies is essential for property owners. The South African property market is influenced by various factors, including local government policies and national economic shifts, which can directly impact tax obligations. Engaging with tax professionals and real estate advisors can provide property owners with tailored strategies that align with their financial goals, ensuring that they remain compliant while maximizing their investment potential. Understanding the dynamic nature of taxes in relation to property ownership is a key component of successful property management and investment in South Africa.

Chapter 12: Security and Safety in Property Management

Importance of Property Security

Property security is an essential aspect of the real estate landscape, particularly in South Africa, where the dynamics of the market can fluctuate significantly. For real estate agents, landlords, and buyers, understanding the importance of robust security measures can not only protect their investments but also enhance the overall value of properties. The rising concerns regarding crime and safety have made it imperative for stakeholders in the property market to prioritize security features when buying, selling, or renting properties. This focus on security not only provides peace of mind but also serves as a selling point that can attract potential buyers and tenants in a competitive market.

In an environment characterized by constantly changing regulations and economic variables, property security has evolved beyond mere physical barriers. Modern security solutions encompass advanced technologies such as electric fencing, surveillance cameras, and smart home systems, which offer enhanced protection and monitoring capabilities. As a result, real estate agents and landlords must stay informed about the latest security technologies and trends to provide their clients with the best advice. By integrating these security features into their properties, stakeholders can significantly reduce vulnerability to theft and vandalism, making properties more appealing and marketable.

Moreover, the role of local government policies in property security cannot be overlooked. Municipalities often implement regulations that affect how properties are secured, such as zoning laws and safety standards. Understanding these policies is crucial for landlords and property managers, as non-compliance can lead to fines and legal issues. Real estate agents must be adept at navigating these regulations to ensure that their clients meet all security requirements while maximizing the property's appeal. Keeping abreast of local government initiatives aimed at enhancing community safety can also provide valuable insights that influence property investment decisions.

The financial implications of property security are significant as well. Properties with advanced security features tend to have higher rental yields and resale values, making them more attractive to investors. For landlords, investing in security enhancements can lead to lower insurance premiums and reduced tenant turnover, ultimately contributing to better financial performance. Buyers should consider the long-term cost benefits of properties equipped with modern security systems, as these features can provide substantial returns on investment. By recognizing the financial advantages of prioritizing property security, stakeholders can make informed decisions that support their success in the market.

In conclusion, the importance of property security in South Africa's dynamic real estate landscape cannot be overstated. With the continuous evolution of market conditions and regulations, real estate agents, landlords, and buyers must adopt a proactive approach to security. By staying informed about the latest trends and technologies, understanding local policies, and recognizing the financial benefits, stakeholders can secure their investments and enhance their market positioning. Ultimately, prioritizing property security is not just about safeguarding assets; it is a strategic move that can yield significant rewards in a competitive and ever-changing environment.

Implementing Effective Security Measures

Implementing effective security measures in the real estate sector is paramount for safeguarding properties, ensuring tenant safety, and enhancing overall marketability. In South Africa, where crime rates can influence buyer sentiment and property values, it becomes essential for real estate agents, landlords, and buyers to prioritize security as a fundamental aspect of property investment and management. This begins with understanding the various security options available, including physical barriers, technological solutions, and community-based strategies that can be tailored to meet the specific needs of each property.

Physical security measures, such as electric fencing and robust locking systems, are often the first line of defines for property owners. Electric fencing not only deters potential intruders but also provides a visible indication of a secure property, which can be a significant selling point for prospective buyers. Additionally, installing high-quality security doors and windows enhances the physical integrity of a home or rental unit, making it less susceptible to break-ins. For landlords, investing in these measures can lead to lower insurance premiums and reduced liability, while also fostering a sense of safety among tenants, which is crucial in retaining them.

Technological advancements have revolutionized property security in recent years. Smart home technologies, including alarm systems, surveillance cameras, and remote monitoring applications, allow property owners to keep a vigilant eye on their investments, even when they are away. These systems can not only respond to security breaches in real-time but can also be integrated with other home automation features, adding convenience and peace of mind for occupants. Real estate agents should highlight these technological enhancements as key selling points when marketing properties, as they reflect a modern approach to safety that resonates with today's buyers and renters.

Community-based security initiatives also play a vital role in promoting safety in residential areas. Neighbourhood watch programs and community policing efforts can foster a sense of collective responsibility among residents, leading to enhanced vigilance and quicker responses to suspicious activities. For landlords and real estate agents, encouraging participation in such initiatives can improve the overall security perception of a property, making it more attractive to potential tenants or buyers. Furthermore, forming relationships with local law enforcement can provide valuable insights into crime trends and effective prevention strategies tailored for specific neighbourhoods.

Finally, compliance with local regulations regarding property security is non-negotiable. With constantly evolving laws and standards, it is crucial for real estate professionals to stay informed about legal requirements related to safety measures in their areas. This includes understanding the implications of municipal rates and taxes that may impact funding for security initiatives, as well as ensuring that all installed systems meet the legal criteria to avoid potential liabilities. By adopting a proactive approach to security measures that encompass physical, technological, and community strategies, real estate agents, landlords, and buyers can navigate the dynamic property landscape with greater confidence and success.

Legal Considerations for Security Systems

Legal considerations for security systems in South Africa's property market are paramount for both landlords and real estate agents. As property owners strive to enhance safety and security measures on their premises, it is essential to navigate the complex web of legal obligations and regulations governing the installation and maintenance of security systems. This includes understanding the requirements set forth by the various acts and regulations that govern property management, such as the Protection of Personal Information Act (POPIA), which impacts how surveillance footage and personal data are handled and stored.

Landlords must ensure that any security measures implemented do not infringe upon tenant rights. This involves a careful balance between maintaining security and respecting the privacy of individuals. For instance, the installation of cameras in communal areas may be permissible, but landlords must inform tenants of their presence and obtain consent where necessary. Additionally, the use of biometric systems or other intrusive technologies can raise legal concerns if they are deemed excessive or invasive, underscoring the necessity for landlords to stay informed about tenant rights and privacy laws.

Furthermore, security systems must comply with local municipal regulations and building codes. This includes ensuring that installations do not violate zoning laws or safety standards. For example, electric fencing, while a popular choice for enhancing property security, must adhere to specific guidelines regarding height, electrification, and signage to avoid legal repercussions. Landlords and real estate agents should proactively consult with local government offices to ensure their security systems meet all regulatory requirements, thus minimizing the risk of fines or legal action.

Insurance considerations also play a critical role in the legal landscape of security systems. Property owners should review their insurance policies to understand how security measures can impact coverage and liability. In some cases, insurers may offer discounts for properties equipped with advanced security systems, while in others, failure to implement adequate security could lead to claims being denied. It is advisable for landlords and real estate agents to engage with insurance professionals to ensure that their policies reflect the current security measures in place and to understand any implications for their coverage.

Lastly, as the property market in South Africa continues to evolve, keeping abreast of changes in legislation and security technologies is vital. Regular training and updates for landlords and real estate agents on legal compliance regarding security systems will help them navigate this dynamic landscape effectively. By prioritizing legal considerations in the implementation of security measures, property owners can not only protect their investments but also foster trust and confidence among tenants, ultimately benefiting all parties involved in the property market.

Chapter 13: The Future of the Property Market

Emerging Trends and Technologies

Emerging trends and technologies are reshaping the real estate landscape in South Africa, presenting both challenges and opportunities for agents, landlords, and buyers. One of the most significant trends is the increasing use of technology in property transactions. Virtual reality and augmented reality tools allow potential buyers to experience properties remotely, providing a more immersive understanding of a space without the need for physical visits. This shift not only enhances the buying experience but also expands the market reach for agents and landlords, allowing them to connect with a broader audience, including international buyers who may be interested in South African properties.

Another notable trend is the growing emphasis on sustainability and green building practices. As environmental concerns rise, buyers are increasingly seeking properties that incorporate eco-friendly features such as solar panels, energy-efficient appliances, and sustainable building materials. This shift is prompting landlords and developers to adapt their strategies, ensuring that their properties meet these new demands. Additionally, government regulations are beginning to reflect this trend, with incentives and subsidies for green initiatives, further encouraging the adoption of sustainable practices in property development and management.

The impact of data analytics on the property market cannot be understated. Agents and investors are leveraging big data to gain insights into market trends, property valuations, and buyer behaviour. By utilizing predictive analytics, they can make informed decisions regarding property investments, pricing strategies, and marketing efforts. This data-driven approach not only enhances the efficiency of real estate transactions but also provides a competitive edge in a fluctuating market. As technology continues to evolve, the integration of artificial intelligence and machine learning will further refine these analytics, enabling more precise forecasting and strategic planning.

The rise of digital platforms for property management and rental agreements has also transformed the landscape. Online property management tools streamline processes such as tenant screening, lease agreements, and maintenance requests, making it easier for landlords to manage their properties efficiently. These platforms often feature automated communication channels that enhance tenant engagement and satisfaction. Furthermore, the ease of accessing legal resources and templates online empowers both landlords and tenants to navigate their rights and responsibilities with greater confidence, fostering a more transparent rental market.

Lastly, the evolving landscape of financing options is crucial for both buyers and investors. Traditional mortgage products are being complemented by innovative financing solutions, such as peer-to-peer lending and crowdfunding platforms. These alternatives provide greater flexibility and accessibility for first-time homebuyers and investors looking to enter the market. As repo rates fluctuate, understanding these financing trends becomes essential for making informed decisions. Staying abreast of these developments not only equips real estate professionals with the knowledge to advise their clients effectively but also positions them to capitalize on emerging opportunities in an ever-changing property market.

Predictions for Market Evolution

The South African property market is poised for significant transformation in the coming years, influenced by a confluence of factors including regulatory changes, economic fluctuations, and shifting consumer preferences. As the government continues to introduce new legislation aimed at improving housing accessibility and affordability, real estate agents and landlords must stay vigilant to ensure compliance and capitalize on opportunities. These evolving regulations could open new avenues for investment and development, particularly in previously neglected areas. Keeping abreast of these changes will be crucial for professionals navigating this dynamic landscape.

Fluctuating interest rates, particularly repo rates, will continue to play a pivotal role in shaping market trends. As the South African Reserve Bank adjusts rates in response to inflationary pressures and economic performance, the cost of borrowing will directly affect buyer sentiment and purchasing power. Real estate agents should be prepared to advise clients on the implications of these shifts, helping them make informed decisions whether they are looking to buy, sell, or invest. A proactive approach to understanding market cycles and financing options will enable agents to better serve their clients and adapt to changes in demand.

Consumer preferences are also evolving, with an increasing focus on sustainability and community-oriented living. Properties that incorporate energy-efficient features or are located near essential services and amenities are likely to see higher demand. Agents and landlords should consider these trends when marketing properties or making investment decisions. Furthermore, the rise of remote work has influenced housing demand, with buyers seeking homes that accommodate flexible lifestyles. Understanding these trends will be essential for stakeholders aiming to align their offerings with market expectations.

In light of these developments, property management practices must evolve to enhance tenant satisfaction and retention. Effective management goes beyond maintenance; it encompasses understanding tenant needs and fostering community engagement. Landlords who prioritize tenant experience through responsive communication, amenities, and community-building initiatives will likely see reduced vacancy rates and increased loyalty. This shift emphasizes the importance of strategic property management in an ever-changing market.

Finally, the impact of local government policies cannot be understated. Zoning regulations, property taxes, and municipal rates influence property values and investment viability. As municipalities strive to address housing shortages and urban development challenges, stakeholders must stay informed about policy changes and their potential repercussions. Engaging with local government initiatives and understanding the broader socio-economic landscape will empower real estate professionals to make strategic decisions that not only benefit their clients but also contribute to sustainable community development.

Preparing for Future Changes in the Property Landscape

The property landscape in South Africa is subject to numerous variables that can shift with little notice, making it essential for real estate agents, landlords, and buyers to remain vigilant and informed. Constantly changing regulations, fluctuating market conditions, and evolving property trends demand a proactive approach to navigate the complexities of the industry. Staying abreast of these changes requires a commitment to continuous learning and adaptation, enabling property professionals to make informed decisions that align with the current market climate.

Understanding the impact of repo rates on the property market is crucial for all stakeholders. These rates directly influence mortgage costs, which in turn affect buyer affordability and demand. A rise in repo rates can lead to a slowdown in property sales, while lower rates may stimulate the market. Real estate agents should monitor these trends closely and provide clients with insights on how changes in the financial landscape could affect their investment strategies. For landlords, adjusting rental prices in line with economic shifts can help maintain occupancy rates and optimize returns on investment.

Navigating the myriads of local and national regulations is another critical aspect of preparing for future changes. Policies regarding property taxes, zoning laws, and tenant rights can dramatically alter the landscape for landlords and real estate professionals. Staying informed about legislative changes and understanding their implications on property management and investment strategies is essential. Attending workshops, engaging with industry associations, and leveraging technology can provide valuable resources for keeping abreast of regulatory updates.

Market analysis plays a pivotal role in anticipating property trends and making strategic decisions. Real estate professionals should utilize data analytics and market research to identify emerging patterns, such as shifts in buyer preferences or demographic changes influencing property demand. By understanding these trends, agents can better advise their clients on timing their purchases or sales, while landlords can optimize their rental strategies to align with market expectations. This informed approach will enhance their competitive edge in a dynamic market.

Lastly, fostering strong relationships with clients and other industry professionals is vital in preparing for future changes. Building a network of trusted contacts, including financial advisors, legal experts, and property management specialists, can provide a comprehensive support system for navigating complex transactions. By collaborating and sharing insights, all parties involved can better anticipate changes and adjust their strategies accordingly. In an ever-evolving property landscape, the ability to adapt and respond to new challenges is essential for long-term success.

More About the Author

Hannes van Zyl was born in Ermelo in the mid-sixties as the first of four siblings. He grew up on farms and enjoyed a healthy childhood. During his schooling years, he lived in a hostel, returning home on weekends and holidays. With his parents often away on business, he spent weekends with his grandparents and holidays with his parents.

After completing school, he joined the Prison Service, where he worked with death row inmates at Pretoria Maximum Prison, studied Psychology, and witnessed executions. After two years, he resigned and served in Panster, Bloemfontein, participating in final operations in Angola.

In the late eighties, he worked as a salesperson in Pretoria and, in the early nineties, started a business with a friend. He relocated to Rustenburg in the mid-nineties to launch a food industry business with his parents, later becoming an estate agent and furthering his studies in Project Management in the late nineties.

Hannes has built a solid professional background, leading high-performing teams with expertise in budgeting, timeline coordination, and risk management. His strengths include effective communication and the ability to collaborate with cross-functional teams while managing multiple projects on time and within budget. With extensive experience in construction management, he excels in project planning and innovative problem-solving, consistently meeting deadlines, staying within budget, and exceeding quality standards.

He is adept at stakeholder collaboration, defining objectives, and ensuring customer satisfaction, demonstrating a results-oriented approach in dynamic environments.

In his thirties, he took on the role of a father figure to two young men, ages 19 and 20, which transformed his life and provided him with renewed purpose. He is also a proud grandfather to three grandchildren. Tragically, his eldest son passed away in a motorcycle accident in late 2023.

As a Property Practitioner, he assists sellers and buyers in marketing and purchasing properties at fair prices, prepares essential paperwork such as contracts and leases, and collaborates with attorneys and lenders to estimate property values.

As a Life Coach and Public Speaker with 20 years of experience, he has helped over 300 clients set and achieve their goals, achieving positive outcomes in 139 out of 140 suicide cases, managing 126 child abuse cases, and realizing an 80% success rate in 189 drug abuse cases. He has authored seven self-help courses and delivered numerous seminars on transformative topics.

As a Project Manager and Director, he co-planned designs for various projects, successfully completing eight estates with 595 *units, all on time and within budget. He also managed the construction of ten luxury homes, overseeing landscaping for these projects.*

In his roles as a Business Administrator and Project Manager, he led teams in planning significant projects like a Retirement Village costing R 195 million and a 90-bed private hospital costing R 576 million. He redesigned a plot into a wedding venue in Pretoria for R 6,500,000.

His diplomas include Project Management, Business Administration, and Structural Engineering, alongside certificates in various fields such as Engineering Management and Public Speaking.

Throughout his life, he has maintained a passion for writing. In late 2024, he decided to pursue writing full-time, aiming to complete over 15 titles he has developed, with many more ideas and stories yet to come.

More Books by the Author

Heartfelt Obedience: Discovering the Blessings of Honouring Parents

The Bible places significant emphasis on the concept of honour, particularly in the context of familial relationships. One of the most well-known commandments regarding honour is found in Exodus 20:12, which states, "Honor your father and your mother, so that you may live long in the land the Lord your God is giving you." This commandment highlights the importance of respecting and valuing one's parents. It establishes a foundational principle that underscores the relationship between children and their parents, suggesting that honouring them is not just a moral obligation but also linked to the well-being and longevity of one's life.

In addition to the commandment in Exodus, the Bible offers various verses that further elaborate on the significance of honouring parents. Proverbs 1:8 encourages children to heed the instruction of their parents, emphasizing the wisdom that can be gained from listening to them. This highlights the idea that honour goes beyond mere obedience; it encompasses actively seeking to learn from parental guidance. By embracing this principle, children can cultivate a deeper appreciation for their parents' *experiences and insights, which can ultimately lead to personal growth and understanding.*

Enduring The Silence: Stories of Hope by Scripture

As we embark on our own journeys of patience and trust, let us draw strength and encouragement from these timeless stories that continue to inspire countless individuals across generations. Each story serves as a reminder that even in our darkest moments, we are not alone; God walks alongside us, guiding us through life's valleys and difficulties. Even in those quiet moments when we might feel isolated and uncertain, God is working in surprising and profound ways, weaving together every experience, challenge, and triumph into a meaningful whole.

By choosing to move forward in faith, we align ourselves with His divine plan, transforming our waiting into a testament of hope and resilience that can uplift and encourage others on their own journeys.

Let us remember that our faith journey isn't solely for our own benefit; it serves as a beacon of hope for those who may be struggling to find their way in life. It illuminates the path through darkness and inspires others to seek truth and light in their own lives, fostering a deeper connection with the divine.

Beyond the Veil: Finding Hope after the Death of a Child

The death of a child is often regarded as the greatest tragedy one can ever experience. There is truly nothing more heartbreaking in life. In addition to the typical symptoms and stages of grief that many individuals face, various factors contribute to the unique and profound challenges of parental bereavement. The immense sorrow stemming from the loss of a child can be further complicated by a deep sense of injustice — the natural feeling that this devastating loss should never have occurred and that no parent should have to endure such pain.

Grief is an incredibly profound experience, one that touches the very core of our being in ways we often cannot articulate, especially when it involves the heartbreaking loss of a child. For many Christians, this journey through grief becomes deeply intertwined with their faith, offering a unique and transformative lens through which to understand the complexities of pain and loss. The nature of grief is multifaceted; it can elicit feelings of deep sorrow, confusion, frustration, and even anger. Yet, within these swirling emotions lies the potential for profound healing, personal growth, and a renewed sense of hope that can emerge over time. By acknowledging the intricate complexity of grief, we can begin to navigate our feelings with greater awareness while holding on to the promises and comfort found in scripture, which can guide us through even the darkest moments.

Behind Closed Doors: The Psychological Impact of Hidden Love

Understanding clandestine relationships requires delving deeply into the intricate and often tumultuous emotional landscape that accompanies loving someone who is already entangled with another person. For individuals who find themselves in such complicated situations, the initial thrill and excitement can rapidly be overshadowed by a multitude of challenges and emotional upheavals. The secrecy that is inherently woven into these relationships frequently fosters a profound sense of isolation, as lovers are compelled to navigate their intense feelings away from the prying eyes of public scrutiny. This hidden existence not only complicates the dynamics of the relationship but can also lead to a significant disconnect from one's true self, ultimately stunting personal growth and severely hindering the ability to form genuine connections with others outside the clandestine affair. The emotional toll can be substantial, leaving individuals grappling with feelings of guilt, longing, and uncertainty about their future.

Second Chances: A Journey Through Faith and Forgiveness

Understanding human fallibility is essential for everyone, regardless of age or background, as we handle the complexities of life and the myriad challenges that come with it. We are all inherently imperfect, prone to mistakes and missteps that shape our experiences. Children might stumble over their words while trying to express themselves, teenagers could make impulsive decisions that lead to valuable lessons, and adults may carry the weight of regrets from the past that inform their present choices. Yet, it is through these very imperfections that we come to appreciate the richness of our journey and the depth of our connections with one another. The Bible teaches us that all have sinned and fall short of the glory of God (Romans 3:23), highlighting our shared nature of fallibility and our collective need for understanding and forgiveness. Recognizing this profound truth allows us to embrace our human condition with grace, humility, and compassion for ourselves and others.

As we take the time to reflect on our shortcomings and the areas where we may have faltered, we also come to recognize the incredible and precious gift of grace that is bestowed upon us. God's grace is defined as unmerited favour, a divine love that forgives and restores us, even in the face of our many flaws and imperfections. In our daily lives, this grace manifests itself through the forgiveness we extend not only to ourselves but also to others around us. When we choose to truly embrace forgiveness, we create a vital space for healing and personal growth. Ephesians 4:32 serves as a powerful reminder for us to be kind and compassionate, urging us to forgive one another just as in Christ, God forgave us. This profound call to forgive empowers us to move forward in our lives, transforming our past failures and mistakes into valuable lessons that deepen our faith and enrich our relationships with others. By accepting grace and practicing forgiveness, we embark on a journey of renewal and connection.

The Silent Struggle: Understanding and Supporting Those Considering the End

Suicidal thoughts frequently arise from a complex interplay of emotional, psychological, and situational factors that can be difficult to untangle. For individuals grappling with these thoughts, it may feel as though they are engulfed in a deep, overwhelming darkness that obscures any sense of hope or joy from their lives. Many may become convinced that they are caught in an unending cycle of pain, with no possible escape, which can intensify feelings of hopelessness and despair. It is vital to understand that these thoughts often serve as a symptom of deeper underlying issues, such as depression, anxiety, or trauma. Recognizing this connection is crucial for seeking help. Moreover, it is essential to acknowledge that these feelings can severely distort one's perception of reality, making it incredibly challenging to see any viable alternatives to the pain they are enduring, leading to a sense of isolation and helplessness that can be overwhelming.

For friends and family members of those who are grappling with suicidal thoughts, it is absolutely vital to approach the situation with deep empathy and compassion. Many individuals may not openly share their feelings, which can lead loved ones to feel helpless and uncertain in how to provide the necessary support. It is essential to cultivate an environment where open and honest conversations about mental health can take place without fear of judgment or stigma. By encouraging individuals to freely express their thoughts and feelings, we can help demystify their experiences and create a safe space for vulnerability that may provide an invaluable opportunity for genuine connection. This connection can serve as a lifeline, reminding those who are in distress that they are not alone in their struggles and that there are people who care deeply about them.

In His Image: Discovering Personal Worth through Faith

Identity is an intricate and multi-faceted concept, shaped by a wide array of elements including personal experiences, core beliefs, and evolving perspectives over time. When considering the aspect of faith, identity transcends the mere social labels we might adopt; it is profoundly influenced by our intimate connection with God. For those of us grappling with profound questions surrounding our worth and purpose in life, recognizing ourselves as being made in God's image provides a foundational and transformative perspective. This divine image not only bestows upon us a sense of intrinsic value and dignity but also inspires us to embrace our unique identities in a manner that is both deeper and more meaningful. It encourages each of us to embark on a fulfilling journey of self-discovery and personal exploration through the enriching lens of spirituality, which, in turn, deepens our connections with God and with one another in a significant way. This journey invites us to reflect on our beliefs and experiences, fostering a richer understanding of ourselves and our place in the world.

Understanding spiritual identity requires a profound and nuanced exploration of the intricate relationship between personal beliefs and the teachings of various faiths. When individuals pose the question, "Who am I in the eyes of God?" they embark on a transformative journey of self-discovery that transcends societal measures of success, achievement, and value. This significant exploration is often profoundly informed by scriptural teachings, which emphasize the vital importance of recognizing oneself as a cherished creation of God. Embracing this perspective nurtures a stronger connection to one's spiritual identity and enables us to fully embrace our authentic selves. As we navigate the complexities of life, this understanding empowers us to live with greater clarity, purpose, and fulfilment, leading to a richer engagement with both our inner selves and the broader world around us. Through this journey, individuals can cultivate a deeper appreciation for their unique spiritual paths and foster meaningful connections with others, enhancing their overall sense of belonging and purpose in the divine tapestry of existence.

Surrendering to God: Embracing Peace Through Serious Health Challenges

The moment a life-threatening diagnosis is delivered can feel like a rupture in reality, shattering the world as you know it into countless fragments. For parents, *friends, and loved ones, the initial shock can quickly spiral into a whirlwind of emotions—fear, disbelief, anger, and profound sorrow. It is entirely natural to feel overwhelmed, grappling with questions that seem utterly unanswerable. In this heart-wrenching moment of crisis, it is essential to remember that you are not alone in this journey. The Lord walks with you in your darkest hours, offering strength, guidance, and comfort through His word. Leaning into your faith during this tumultuous time can be a source of profound peace, reminding you that even amidst the chaos and uncertainty, God reigns supreme and is ever-present in your life. Trust that He is there to carry you through the storm.*

As you navigate the tumultuous waters of a serious illness, it may be immensely beneficial to turn to Scripture for both guidance and solace during this challenging time. Verses that speak to God's unwavering presence, such as Psalm 46:1—"God is our refuge and strength, an ever-present help in trouble"—can provide the profound reassurance needed to face the myriad challenges that lie ahead. Embracing these powerful words can truly transform your perspective, allowing you to see your circumstances not merely as a trial to endure, but as a unique opportunity for deeper reliance on God's promises and faithfulness. Engaging in Biblical meditation can further enhance this vital process, helping to quiet the storm within and anchor your spirit in His lasting peace, providing you with strength and comfort during difficult days.

The Dynamic Property Landscape: Strategies for Success in a Changing Market

The South African property market presents a complex landscape shaped by a myriad of factors that affect both residential and commercial real estate. This market is defined by its dynamic nature, with constant shifts in regulations, economic conditions, and property trends. Real estate agents, landlords, and buyers must remain acutely aware of these changes to navigate successfully. The evolving legal framework, often influenced by local government policies, plays a critical role in shaping market conditions, impacting everything from property valuations to investment strategies.

In recent years, fluctuations in the economy have contributed to a volatile property market. The repo rate, set by the South African Reserve Bank, serves as a crucial indicator of borrowing costs, directly influencing mortgage rates and, consequently, buyer affordability. As interest rates rise or fall, the demand for properties can shift dramatically. Buyers must stay informed about these changes, as understanding *the implications of repo rate adjustments can significantly affect their purchasing decisions and overall market engagement.*

Distance and Disconnection: The Hidden Struggles of Christian Men Away from Home

The modern work landscape has undergone significant changes, particularly with the rise of globalization and technological advancement. Many Christian men find themselves in roles that require them to travel extensively or relocate for work, often resulting in physical separation from their families. This shift has created a unique set of challenges, as these men grapple with the demands of their careers while attempting to maintain their roles as husbands and fathers. The distance can lead to emotional isolation, making it difficult for them to stay engaged with their families and uphold their spiritual commitments, which are central to their identities.

For families of Christian men working far from home, the impact of absentee fatherhood is profound. Children may struggle with feelings of abandonment, while wives often bear the burden of managing household responsibilities alone. This dynamic can hinder children's spiritual development, as they miss out on the guidance and presence of their fathers during formative years. The absence of a father figure can lead to confusion regarding faith and values, ultimately affecting the family's overall spiritual health. The challenge lies in maintaining a sense of unity and shared faith, even when physical presence is compromised

The Power Dynamics: Exploring the Top and Bottom Division

The concept of "top" and "bottom" within the gay community often extends far beyond the simplistic notion of mere sexual roles, encompassing a much broader spectrum of identity, power dynamics, and interpersonal relationships. For many individuals within the gay community, these labels can carry a significant amount of weight, profoundly influencing not only how they perceive themselves but also how they are perceived by others in social contexts. The binary classification of these roles can create an environment laden with expectations and pressures, where individuals may feel an obligation to conform to specific roles based on various factors, including their personality traits, physical appearance, or age. This societal perspective can lead to a limited and narrow understanding of identity, ultimately constraining personal expression and authenticity, thereby inhibiting individuals from fully exploring and embracing their true selves.

Growing up, many gay individuals face an overwhelming barrage of perceptions from both within and outside the gay community. Young gay individuals often feel intense pressure to conform to societal archetypes of being a "top" or a "bottom," which are frequently dictated by stereotypes that associate certain personality traits and behaviours with these roles. For instance, those who are perceived as more feminine may be pushed toward the bottom role, while those who exhibit more masculine traits are often expected to take on the top role. This societal pressure can create a profound sense of dissonance for those who do not naturally align with these stereotypes, leading to internalized homophobia, feelings of inadequacy, and a struggle with self-identity. The societal call to "be yourself" can feel profoundly contradictory when societal norms impose such rigid and limiting expectations. This dissonance can further complicate the journey of self-acceptance for many young gay individuals.

When Shadows Wisper: Embracing the Devil's Bargain

Understanding the Devil's Bargain often requires a deep dive into the motivations that drive individuals to make choices that seem counterintuitive. It's essential to recognize that this concept is not solely about succumbing to temptation but also about the complex interplay of circumstances, desires, and the human spirit's resilience. Each of us faces moments when the allure of an easier path beckons, especially when we feel abandoned or isolated. Acknowledging this temptation is the first step toward empowerment, allowing us to choose wisely rather than out of desperation.

In many narratives, the Devil's Bargain symbolizes a moment of weakness, a choice made in the heat of turmoil. However, it is crucial to reframe this understanding. Life can often feel like a series of trials, and in those moments, we may feel that all hope is lost. The devil, represent the struggles we face—fear, loneliness, and despair. Yet, it is within this darkness that we can find the strength to rise above the challenges. Embracing the struggle can lead to profound personal growth and a deeper understanding of our values and what we truly hold dear.

www.ingramcontent.com/pod-product-compliance
Lightning Source LLC
Chambersburg PA
CBHW052321220526
45472CB00001B/215

* 9 7 9 8 3 0 0 0 9 5 3 9 0 *